Arizona

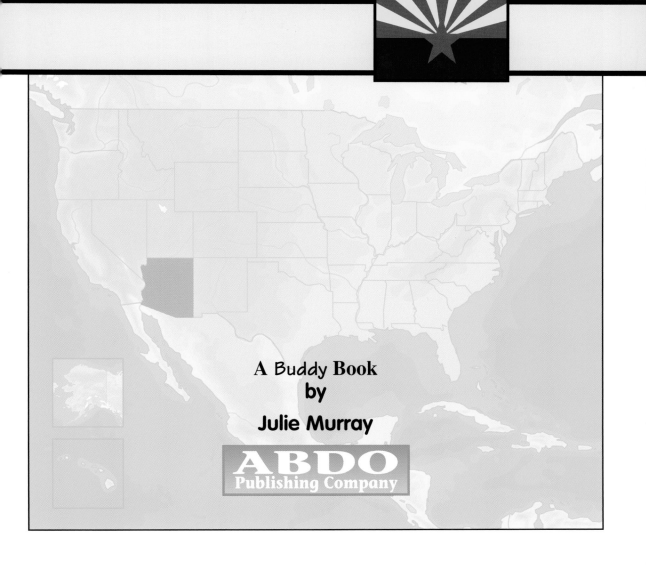

A Buddy Book
by
Julie Murray

ABDO
Publishing Company

VISIT US AT

www.abdopub.com

Published by ABDO Publishing Company, 4940 Viking Drive, Edina, Minnesota 55435.

Printed in the United States.

Edited by: Sarah Tieck
Contributing Editor: Michael P. Goecke
Graphic Design: Deb Coldiron, Maria Hosley
Image Research: Sarah Tieck
Photographs: clipart.com, Corbis, EyeWire, Library of Congress, One Mile Up, Photos.com

Library of Congress Cataloging-in-Publication Data

Murray, Julie, 1969-
    Arizona / Julie Murray.
        p. cm. — (The United States)
    Includes bibliographical references and index.
    ISBN 1-59197-662-6
        1. Arizona—Juvenile literature. I. Title.

F811.3.M87 2005
979.1—dc22

                                                    2004041083

Table Of Contents

A Snapshot Of Arizona

Arizona became an official state on February 14, 1912. It is the 48th state. There are 50 states in the United States.

The Grand Canyon is
277 miles (446 km) long.

Every state is different. Every state has an official state nickname. Arizona is known as "the Grand Canyon State." This is because the Grand Canyon is located in northwestern Arizona. It is one of the Seven Natural Wonders of the World.

Arizona has 114,007 square miles (295,277 sq km) of land. Only five states are bigger. There are 5,130,632 people who live in Arizona. The state ranks 20th in population size.

Many people live in the cities of Arizona.

Where Is Arizona?

There are four parts of the United States. Each part is called a region. Each region is in a different area of the country. The United States Census Bureau says the four regions are the Northeast, the South, the Midwest, and the West.

The state of Arizona is located in the West region of the United States. The weather in most of Arizona is warm and dry. This is because much of southern Arizona is desert. Arizona also has mountains and forests.

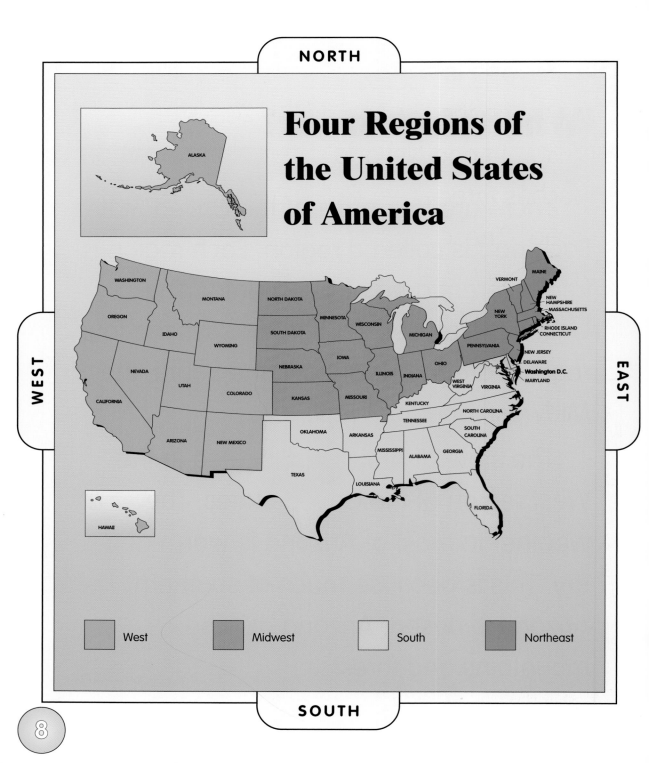

Four Regions of the United States of America

NORTH

WEST

EAST

SOUTH

ALASKA

WASHINGTON
MONTANA
NORTH DAKOTA
MINNESOTA
VERMONT
MAINE
OREGON
IDAHO
SOUTH DAKOTA
WISCONSIN
MICHIGAN
NEW YORK
NEW HAMPSHIRE
MASSACHUSETTS
WYOMING
IOWA
PENNSYLVANIA
RHODE ISLAND
CONNECTICUT
NEVADA
NEBRASKA
ILLINOIS
INDIANA
OHIO
NEW JERSEY
DELAWARE
UTAH
COLORADO
KANSAS
MISSOURI
WEST VIRGINIA
VIRGINIA
Washington D.C.
MARYLAND
CALIFORNIA
KENTUCKY
ARIZONA
NEW MEXICO
OKLAHOMA
ARKANSAS
TENNESSEE
NORTH CAROLINA
SOUTH CAROLINA
MISSISSIPPI
ALABAMA
GEORGIA
TEXAS
LOUISIANA
FLORIDA

HAWAII

West   Midwest   South   Northeast

8

Arizona is bordered by the country of Mexico to the south, and the states of California and Nevada to the west. Arizona touches three other states at its northeast corner. These states are Utah, Colorado, and New Mexico. This area is called the "Four Corners."

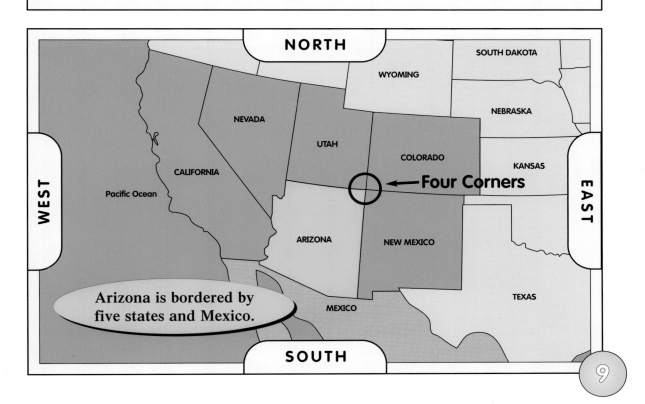

NORTH

SOUTH DAKOTA

WYOMING

NEVADA

NEBRASKA

UTAH

COLORADO

KANSAS

CALIFORNIA

← Four Corners

Pacific Ocean

WEST

EAST

ARIZONA

NEW MEXICO

Arizona is bordered by
five states and Mexico.

MEXICO

TEXAS

SOUTH

Arizona

State abbreviation: AZ

State nickname: The Grand Canyon State

State capital: Phoenix

State motto: Ditat deus (Latin for "God enriches")

Statehood: February 14, 1912, 48th state

Population: 5,130,632, ranks 20th

State flag:
Adopted in 1917

Land area: 114,007 square miles (295,277 sq km), ranks 6th

State tree: Paloverde

State song: "Arizona March Song"

State government: Three branches: legislative, executive, and judicial

Average July temperature: 80°F (27°C)

Average January temperature: 41°F (5°C)

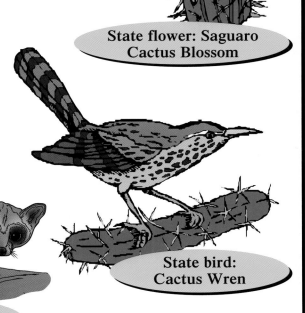

State flower: Saguaro Cactus Blossom

State bird: Cactus Wren

State animal: Ringtail

Cities And The Capital

Phoenix is the largest city in Arizona. It is also the sixth-largest city in the United States. It is Arizona's capital. Phoenix is located in southern Arizona. The city of Phoenix is named for a bird in myths.

The phoenix is a bird. It is in many old stories.

A view of Phoenix.

A view of Tucson.

Tucson is the second-largest city in Arizona. More than 480,000 people live in this city in southern Arizona. Many people like to visit Tucson because it is warm and sunny. It is in a large desert surrounded by mountains. In 1692, Eusebio Francisco Kino opened the San Xavier del Bac Mission near Tucson.

The outside (top) and inside (bottom)
of the San Xavier del Bac Mission.

Famous Citizens

Sandra Day O'Connor (1930–)

Sandra Day O'Connor was born in El Paso, Texas. But, she was an important citizen of Arizona. She was a state senator and a judge there. But, she is famous for being the first woman on the United States Supreme Court. President Ronald Reagan appointed her in 1981. As a Supreme Court judge, Sandra Day O'Connor helps make important decisions.

Sandra Day O'Connor

Famous Citizens

Geronimo (1829–1909)

Geronimo was a Chiricahua Apache. He lived in Arizona. He was known as a warrior. He led a fight against the United States. He was fighting to help the Native Americans in the southwestern United States. The United States government was making the Native Americans live in certain areas. But, the Native Americans wanted to choose where they would live.

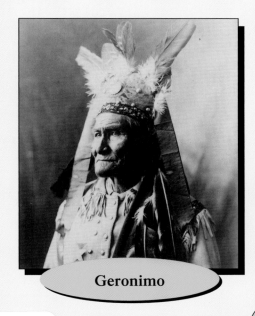

Geronimo

The Grand Canyon

Most of the land in northern Arizona is made up of plateaus and canyons. The Grand Canyon is in this part of Arizona. It is 277 miles (446 km) long. In some places, the canyon is 18 miles (29 km) wide. The Grand Canyon is about one mile (1.6 km) deep.

The Grand Canyon

Grand Canyon National Park was created in 1919. Today, almost 5 million people visit the Grand Canyon each year. They learn about the history and the landscape. It has many activities for people of all ages. People hike, bike, camp, and look at the canyon.

Many people visit the Grand Canyon.

The Painted Desert

The Painted Desert

The Painted Desert is part of a plateau region along the Little Colorado River. It is almost 200 miles (320 km) long.

The land in the Painted Desert is shaped by wind and rain.

Spanish explorers named the Painted Desert. They named it for the rocks that are colored blue, red, purple, and yellow. Heat and light make the colors look different.

There are many colors in the Painted Desert.

Saguaro Cactus

The Saguaro cactus is the largest cactus in the United States. It is sometimes called "the giant cactus." This type of cactus only grows in parts of California, Mexico, and Arizona. In Arizona, it is found in deserts and hills. It is found in the Sonora Desert. The Saguaro cactus blossom is the state flower of Arizona.

The Saguaro cactus blossom

The Saguaro cactus grows in the desert.

Saguaros can grow to be 60 feet (18 m) tall. Some weigh ten tons (nine t). The trunk of a Saguaro can be almost three feet (one m) wide. The Saguaro stores water in this trunk.

The Saguaro cactus grows to be very tall.

Arizona

1539: Marcos de Niza comes to Arizona. He was a priest.

1540: Francisco Coronado comes from Spain to explore Arizona.

1821: Arizona becomes part of Mexico.

1846: The United States goes to war with Mexico.

1848: Mexico gives Arizona to the United States. This happens after the Mexican–American War ends.

1889: Phoenix becomes the capital of Arizona.

1912: Arizona becomes the 48th state on February 14.

1930: Clyde W. Tombaugh discovers Pluto. He was searching from the Lowell Observatory in Flagstaff.

The Hoover Dam

1936: The Hoover Dam is finished.

1981: Sandra Day O'Connor is the first woman to be appointed to the Supreme Court. She was a judge in Arizona.

1988: The St. Louis Cardinals football team moves to Arizona and becomes the Arizona Cardinals.

1994: Grand Canyon celebrates 75 years as a national park.

Cities in Arizona

Flagstaff

★ Phoenix

● Tucson

Important Words

appoint to choose someone to do a job.

canyon a long, narrow valley between two cliffs.

capital a city where government leaders meet.

nickname a name that describes something special about a person or a place.

plateau a flat-topped mountain.

Web Sites

To learn more about Arizona, visit ABDO Publishing Company on the World Wide Web. Web site links about Arizona are featured on our Book Links page. These links are routinely monitored and updated to provide the most current information available.

www.abdopub.com

Index